# Creepy Crawly CRITTERS

## and Other Halloween Tongue Twisters

### by Nola Buck

### pictures by Sue Truesdell

HarperTrophy
*A Division of* HarperCollins*Publishers*

CREEPY CRAWLY CRITTERS
*and other Halloween Tongue Twisters*
Text copyright © 1995 by Nola Buck
Illustrations copyright © 1995 by Susan G. Truesdell
Printed in the U.S.A.  All rights reserved.

Library of Congress Cataloging-in-Publication Data
Buck, Nola.
  Creepy crawly critters and other Halloween tongue twisters / by Nola
Buck ;  illustrated by Sue Truesdell.
       p.       cm. — (An I can read book.)
   ISBN 0-06-024808-4. — ISBN 0-06-024809-2 (lib. bdg.)
ISBN 0-06-444222-5 (pbk.)
   1. Tongue twisters.   2. Halloween—Juvenile literature.   3. Animals—
Juvenile literature.   [1. Tongue twisters.   2. Halloween.   3. Animals.
4. Insects.]   I. Truesdell, Sue, ill.   II. Title.   III. Series.
PN6371.5.B83   1995                                                     94-15405
818'.5402—dc20                                                              CIP
                                                                            AC

❖
First Harper Trophy edition, 1996

*For Charlotte Rashti,*
*critter extraordinaire!*
*—N.B.*

*For Cynthia*
*—S.T.*

Glad ghosts groan.

5

Glowing goblins gleam.

6

Two tree toads try

trick-or-treating too.

Slow sly snakes slither silently.

A pirate picked a pair

of pretty purple pants.

10

Which silk shoes did Sue choose?

Bob's boys bob in a big black bucket.

Is Ruth's tooth loose?

Shy spiders sing slow sad songs.

Eight ants dance in Aunt Pat's pants.

Itty-bitty bats bit big bad bedbugs.

Creepy crawly critters keep quiet.

Brenda blew big blue bubbles.

A rat bit a cat

who bit a bat

who bit a rat.

20

Pass a piece of pumpkin pie, please.

21

Flies fly free.

Fleas flee flies.

Which witch's britches itch?

A spider spied her apple cider.

Slowly sipped it there beside her.

Sadly, slipped into the punch,

Becoming apple spider lunch.

Blair bumped Burt.

Burt burped.

Plump pumpkins play.

Shy Sally slides slyly

in shiny silver slippers.

Tricky trick-or-treaters
try trading sticky treats.

Trudy chewed two treats twice.

Cross crows cried *CAW!*

31

Ten tomcats tell ten tall tales.